SUMMER HOUSES OF KENDAL

SUMMER HOUSES OF KENDAL

DAVID M. BUTLER

with a foreword by ALEC CLIFTON-TAYLOR

ABBOT HALL
ART GALLERY
KENDAL
1982

ACKNOWLEDGEMENTS

I would like to record my thanks to the Curwen Archives Trust whose generous grant has made possible the publication of this book.

I have been much helped in the course of its preparation by the staff of the County Records Office and the Kendal Local History Library, and by many friends.

I am grateful too for the contribution made by the printers, who have persuaded my miscellaneous collection of material into a unified and attractive book.

Printed in Great Britain by Titus Wilson Ltd., Kendal

ISBN 0 9503335 2 2

FOREWORD

The longer I live, the more certain I become that we can never stop discovering new architectural pleasures in England. Until I read Mr. Butler's study, I had no idea that Kendal had such a proliferation of summer houses – or, as many would term them, gazebos. I doubt whether any other English town had half the number: not many towns, of course, offer such inviting distant prospects at which to gaze! It is sad that several have been lost in recent years. I very much hope that the few which remain will all be preserved.

It is a pleasure to introduce Mr. Butler's interesting study of them, and to say how much I admire, too, his charming drawings. He has also provided an indispensable map and several relevant sections of old town plans. The people of Kendal are very lucky to be offered this account, exactly the right length, of what the author calls a 'little known backwater' of the history of their town.

ALEC CLIFTON-TAYLOR,
O.B.E., F.S.A., HON. F.R.I.B.A.

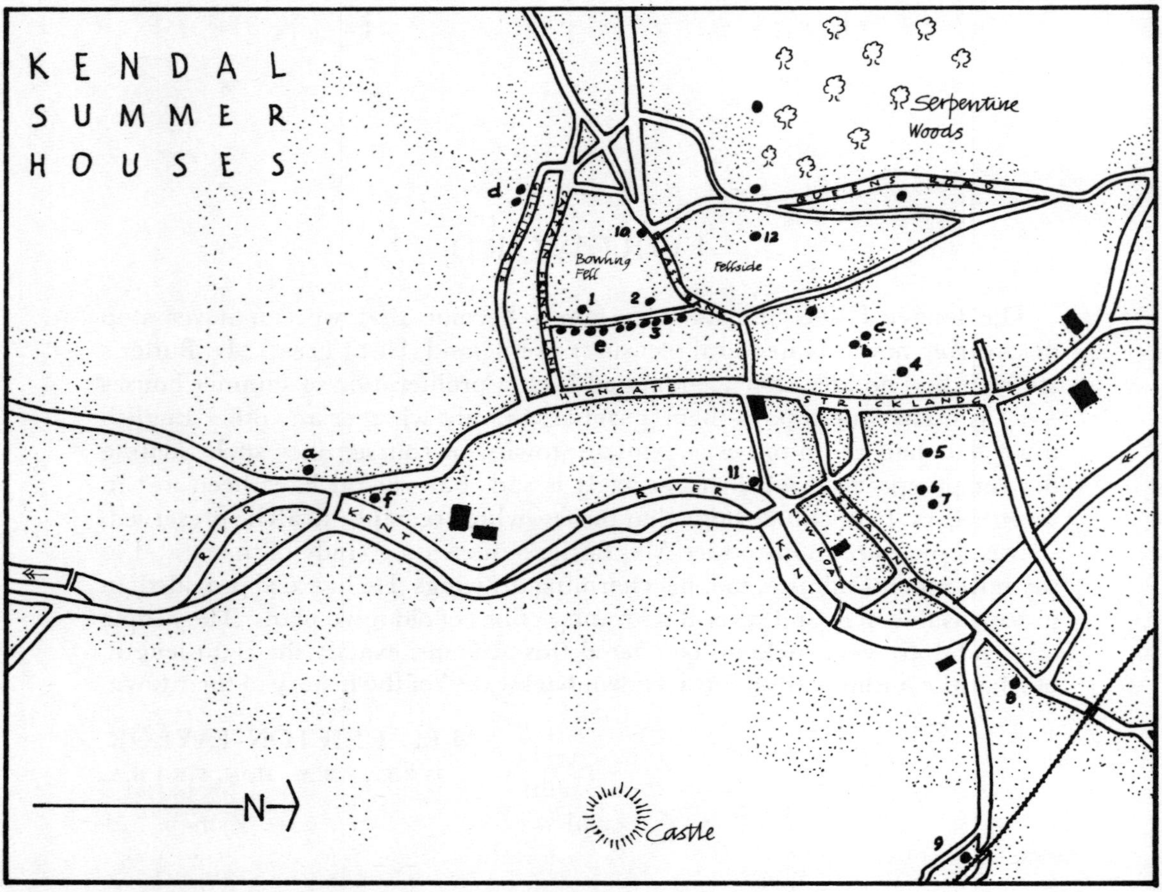
KENDAL
SUMMER
HOUSES
Serpentine
Woods
QUEENS ROAD
Bowling Fell
Fellside
HIGHGATE
STRICKLANDGATE
RIVER
KENT
RIVER
NEW ROAD
KENT
STRAMONGATE
N
Castle

SUMMER HOUSES OF KENDAL

The Kendal of two centuries ago may be pictured as a lively and compact town, busy and prosperous. It was then, as it still is, an irregular collection of buildings on irregular ground. Houses, shops, workshops and warehouses stood 'back to back, corner to corner, some up-hill, some down, without intent or meaning' as a visitor in 1769 wrote in his journal. Around these buildings the air was full of the smoke of countless fires burning peat from Milnthorpe or Lyth. Open country was not far away though, and between the rough smoke-blackened walls there were glimpses of Benson Knot and the Helm across the river to the east, or of Kendal Fell rising close upon the western side of the town. Along the main streets substantial houses were packed close, and gracing their long steep narrow gardens were summer houses which are the subject of these notes. Here above the hurry and the smoke the family could escape to enjoy peace and the distant view.

homas Grey

These were no transient flights of fancy made up of bark-covered boughs or lath and plaster, but good stone buildings which were intended for use as well as for decoration. They were special to Kendal which surpassed other towns in the number and the quality of its summer houses, in the excellence of their accommodation and the substance of their construction. There was not anything very special in the situation or the circumstances of the town, yet the combination of factors was right for the exceptional development of these buildings, and one does not see their equal elsewhere.

These summer houses were a substantial part of substantial properties, belonging to the homes of professional men and well-to-do tradesmen and men of business. They were regular in form and small in scale, and in the details of their design they often bore some similarity to the house in front. The materials they were made of were the same: limestone from the quarries on Kendal Fell and pale green slate brought in from a few miles north. A two-storey summer house was the rule rather than the exception at the upper end of the scale, a scale which diminished through smaller and single-storey buildings to open alcoves, albeit still of substantial construction. At this lower level and with buildings which have stood derelict for one or two generations it might be thought difficult to distinguish summer house from garden shed. There are some buildings with the outward appearance of the latter which on closer inspection are seen to have their floor raised well above the ground and their window a good deal larger than mere utility dictates, which are thus brought into the same group as others which were built for pleasure first and usefulness after. Those with two floors generally gave one level to each function. The upper room was reached by stone steps lined by a slight wrought-iron handrail, inside it the accommodation and the finishes were almost domestic in standard. Some had a wall-cupboard perhaps for a rack of pipes and a pair of tankards, several a fireplace against the chill of an autumn evening, some a plaster cornice and decorative arched recesses in the thickness of the walls. Whatever else the summer house offered there was a fine large sash window giving a view of the eastern fells across the town lit by the low evening sun.

When these summer houses were built the citizens of Kendal occupied the traditional burgage properties: deep narrow plots of land whose boundaries had been set out many years earlier. One is described in 1731: 'To be sold, a very good Burgage house, Stable, Cow-house, Tan-yard, Bark-mill and garden late belonging to Stanley Brockbank and situate in Kirkland, near Kendal'. Curwen brought this notice up-to-date in 1900 – 'This tan-yard was on the south side of Poor House Lane, where there is now an extensive garden and summer house'; more recent change has lost us this garden and the town's southernmost summer house. The proprietor of such a burgage property lived with his family in the house on the street front and ran his trade from workshop or warehouse behind; beyond these, where the ground rose more steeply, was his garden. Old plans of the town show how little these plots have changed, and until recently they were seldom combined or sub-divided. The owner would develop his property within the old-established boundaries, either for profit by building workshops or worker's houses thus forming the now traditional yards, or for pleasure by improving his garden with fruit-trees, terraces, flights of steps and a summer house. Thus as Kendal prospered it increased in density rather than extent and by so doing it still further increased the enjoyment which these little buildings offered.

Curwen, *Kirkbie Kendal*, 1900, p. 189

letter 'a' on map

Of course not all Kendalians inhabited such well-provided premises and many who lived in the yards and side streets had to grow their vegetables in one of the several Common Gardens situated around the town at this period from the slopes of Castle Hill to the land above All Hallows Lane. Others were better off but were still without gardens: residents of the more closely-packed areas around Finkle Street and the Market Place bought their own detached garden on the edge of the town. This is illustrated by a memorandum of 1776 recording the purchase for £15. 5s. 0d. of 'all that Garden with a Summer House standing therein, . . . being on the Fellside in Kirkbie Kendal'. It had been bought by James Fell, an apothecary and surgeon who lived and practised in Finkle Street and who died in 1803. The precise location of his garden has not been identified, however another such is known with certainty, a detached garden and summer house which had been established about 1780 on one corner of Bowling Fell. Both these gardens were some way from home, where pleasant and useful shelter was all the more desirable; thus they might suggest the origin of this fashion for summer houses which became so popular in the town. The one on Bowling Fell shows near perfection in its situation and equipment, and must have represented the ultimate wish of local people in the furnishing of their garden.

Parish Church Registers

See p. 9

To these domestic uses may be added another, or rather another type of building may be added which is scarcely distinguishable in appearance from a summer-house. Several inns in Kendal as of course elsewhere included a bowling green among the pleasures which they afforded their customers, greens which were sometimes provided with buildings to give shelter to the players and to house their bowls, and which here were like summer houses in all respects but the view from the window. One of these belonged to the Woolpack and lay on the opposite side of Entry Lane from the inn, it is shown as a bowling green on town plans of 1787 and 1833. Both these, and the later plan of 1853 show the small club-house attached to the green, centrally at its eastern end. The walls which once enclosed this green still stand, but it and the club house have gone and small workshops stand in their place. This inn had incidentally another summer house attached, mentioned in a conveyance dated 1786, a 'garden and summer house on the north side of Entry Lane, belonging to the Woolpack Inn'. The building was fairly new then, for the earlier deed of 1750 does not mention it. When the Wheat Sheaf Inn in Kirkland changed hands in 1833 a 'Spacious Bowling Green' was mentioned in the notice of sale: it lay between the inn and Kirkbarrow House. There was once a green too at the top of Beast Bank, successor to one on Bowling Fell, this one not so obviously related to an inn but provided with a very pleasant club house which will be described later.

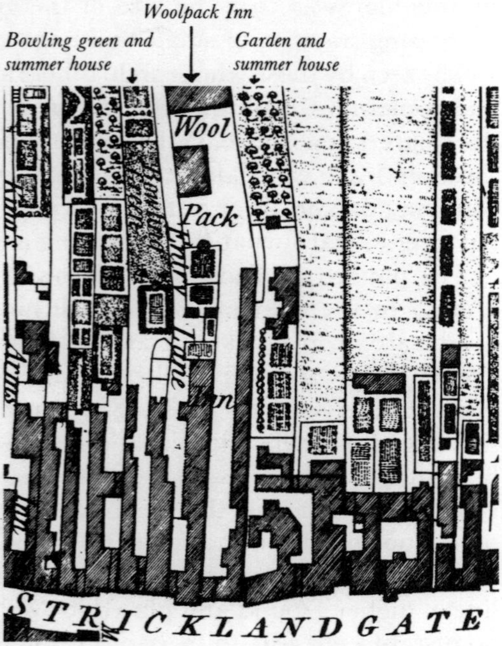

Todd, 1787

tter 'b'
n map

.R.O. ref.
/D/W

tter 'c'
n map

ee p. 11

The period of Kendal summer houses began well before the last quarter of the eighteenth century when William Gilpin and Thomas Gray published their accounts of journeys in the Lakes which drew tourists in search of the picturesque; thus confirming the suggestion that their origin is not to be sought in outside influences but rather within Kendal itself. They were firmly established in the life of the town by 1750 and a century later the vogue had pretty well passed, though still towards the end of the nineteenth century as new houses were built outside the limits of the old town, so were new summer houses built as well, perpetuating the local tradition of a well provided garden.

89, 1775

There is firm evidence for at least thirty summer houses within Kendal, with more only hinted at and still to be clearly defined. Their usual location on the back wall of the garden means that very few can be seen from public thoroughfares so that the size of the group is not easily realised. An ever-decreasing number of small buildings and even smaller piles of rubble may still be seen by those who search, others are known only from written references and sometimes confirmed by old plans of the town. More than half of the thirty are known to have been the substantial buildings already described, three at least were alcoves of stone and slate, two were of heavy timber construction and three or four we know were not up to the local standard; we have yet to learn what the remaining few were like.

The pattern of distribution shows a well-marked sweep along the higher ground to the west of the town turning east through its centre. They run northward from Kirkland and are most closely packed between Captain French Lane and All Hallows Lane where there was a summer house on average every thirty yards. Further north they are less regularly placed because of the different formation of the land and several may have been lost here through the more varied and changing use of the area. At the highest part of Stricklandgate their line crosses the road to follow the back of properties on the north side of Stramongate, continuing less distinctly across the river to Wildman Street. A few more summer houses were placed either side of this line of higher ground and placed as well as their situation allowed even when no distant view was to be had. Of the thirty we know of, about twenty were built to this first pattern. The remainder were constructed in the period from the early years of the last century in the more spacious new gardens on the edge of the town; not as a clearly defined second phase but rather as the later stages of a continuous growth. The process is well demonstrated at the large house Lynnside which was built on Gillinggate less than a century ago and was provided with 'one good Summer House with large windows, one open Summer House'.

letter 'd' on map

particulars of sale, 1942

Bradley Field.

It might be asked whether this concentration of summer houses in the town has been reflected in the surrounding countryside, and it is quite possible that there are more in the immediate district than would otherwise be the case. On the edge of the town in Serpentine Woods a summer house was built in 1833 or 1834, octagonal, and with windows overlooking the valley in the Woods. It was one of the attractions of the Woods and one which every Kendalian would expect to find; the key was available to those who wished to use it for picnics. At this period between 1827 and 1849 the Woods were not freely open but admission was by a charge of sixpence. Where else in the Kingdom was one offered a summer house for hire by the afternoon? It still stands, restored by Kendal Civic Society, and open to all. A little further outside the town off the road to Underbarrow at Boundary Bank is one rather in the French chateau style (as are some of the houses of a similar mid-nineteenth century date in and around Kendal), tall and with a steeply-pitched roof. At Whitefoot beyond Burneside is one more ornate than most with a decorative weather-vane; on the side of the Helm is another, unusually simple of 'art and craft' origin, a plain drum with a conical roof: from a distance appearing as a slate roof but made largely of concrete. More important than any of these, because it is contemporary with the original group in the town, is the summer house at Bradley Field House, over a mile to the west of Kendal. This is a square stone building with a slated pyramid roof, a fireplace and two windows, set at the end of a raised and tree-lined terrace.

Trustees' Minutes

Serpentine Woods.

Boundary Bank.

High Wells, Helm.

All the summer houses which have been located and identified with a fair degree of certainty are shown on the map, which leaves aside a few ruins of buildings of less

Bradley Field.

certain use and takes no account of many other small black squares in gardens shown on the old town plans. These old surveys show well the pattern of distribution and illustrate its growth as survey succeeds survey. They have to be used with caution however as not all are equally carefully prepared away from the main street frontages. The earliest to be of any use at all for this purpose is Thomas Jeffrey's survey of 1770. John Todd's plan of 1787, John Wood's of 1833 and Henry Hoggarth's of 1853 all show the town to a larger scale and with considerable detail. More still is to be found on the sheets of the 1:500 scale Ordnance Survey made in 1851, where each back yard and garden path is carefully set down.

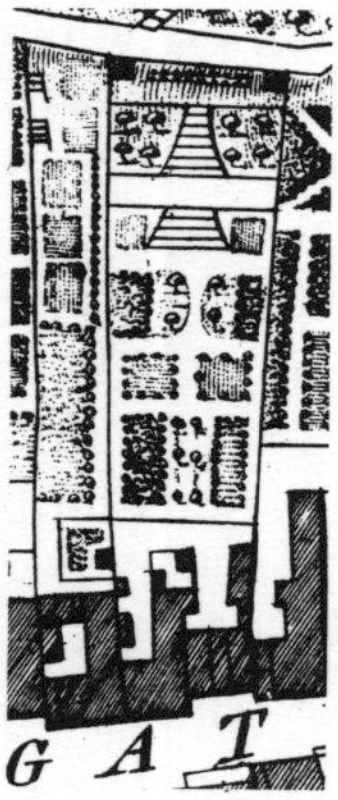

Todd, 1787

letter 'e' on map

Nicholson, *Annals of Kendal*, 1861, p. 296

These plans show for instance the large house immediately to the south of the Brewery in Highgate, once the home of Isaac Braithwaite, with behind it the impressive flights of steps which diminish in width as they rise through the terraces of the garden where are shown two summer houses, one each end of the upper terrace. We can still walk through that garden and up those fine steps to the upper terrace, but once there we do not see the buildings; only by being so guided by the map might we notice the slight remains of two timber summer houses, no doubt successors to those shown on the old plans. Another map shows a summer house near the entrance to the Vicarage grounds, the old vicarage that was situated between the parish church and Nether Bridge. It was noted in the Annals of Kendal for 1825-6 that 'the Rev. J. Hudson removed the tan yards near the Vicarage,

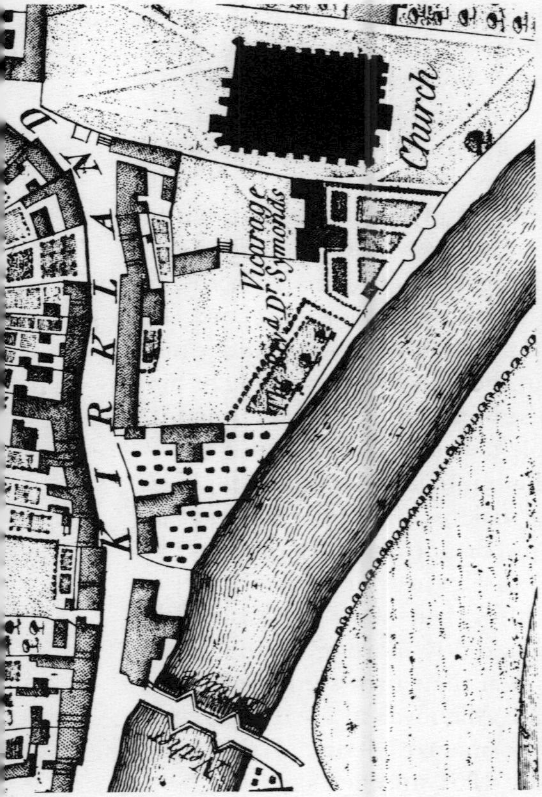

'odd, 1787: tan pits.

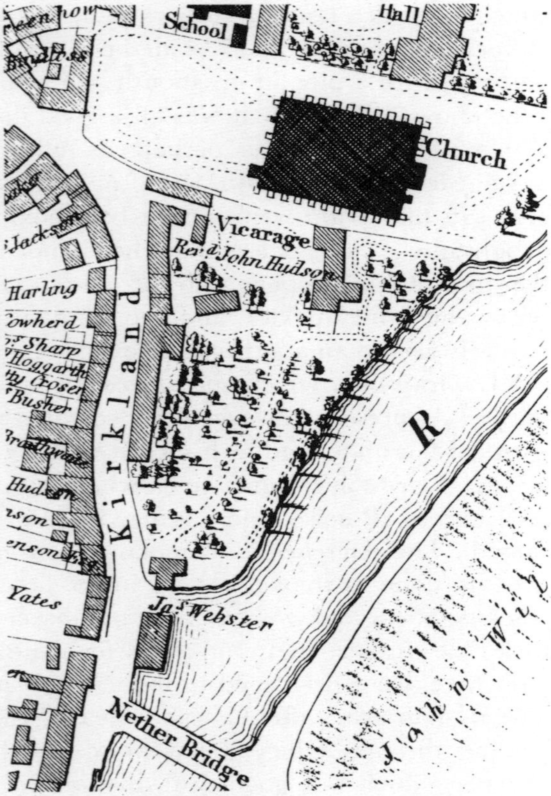

Wood, 1833: Vicarage garden.

built a neat lodge and adorned the grounds'. Todd's map shows the tan-pits, and the map of 1851 shows lodge and drive with a summer house at the end of the river-side walk. We look now in vain for these adornments, finding little but an old decorative tree.

etter 'f'
n map

These summer houses, gazebos or whatever, were taken so much for granted that no one appears to have left us any description of their part in the life of the town. Elsewhere in the country a few such references occur, and authors or travellers occasionally made mention of the delight they offered. Shakespeare for instance refers to a summer house as a token of high life, while Daniel Defoe on his travels through Britain around 1725 described his host's 'duckery, which is an oval pond bricked round, and his pretty summer house by it, in

Hy IV part 1,
. 1

Cowper's Summer House, Olney, Bucks.

which to drink a bottle'. To Dickens it was an adjunct to Sam Weller's hopes of social advancement: 'I shall be a gentleman myself one of these days perhaps, with a pipe in my mouth and a summer-house in the back garden. Who knows?' To a few it was all a good deal more important, and the poet William Cowper gave us perhaps as full a picture as any when he wrote 'I have at length, my cousin, found my way into my summer abode . . . I will only say that I am writing in a bandbox, situated at least in my account, delightfully . . .' 'It is a summerhouse not much bigger than a sedan chair, the door of which opens into the garden which is now crowded with roses, pinks and honeysuckles, and the window into my neighbour's orchard. It formerly served an apothecary, now dead, as a smoking-room, and under my feet is a trap-door which once covered a hole in the ground where he kept his bottles. At present however it is dedicated to sublimer uses. Having lined it with garden mats, and furnished it with a table and two chairs, here I write all that I write in summer-time, whether to the public or to my friends. It is secure from all noise, and a refuge from all intrusions . . . A poet's retreat is sacred'. The reference to a smoking-room is important, for at that period it was not done to smoke tobacco in the house: the highest in the land had a smoking room and a velvet smoking jacket within their mansion; lesser folk took that pleasure in an inn. Very few, and apparently more in Kendal than elsewhere, were privileged to indulge in a pipe in their own summer house. Twenty-four years after Cowper's death William Allen was in the district; 'In passing through Olney, he went to see the former residence of the Poet Cowper, which is a good deal dilapidated'. By 1851 another sightseer 'felt great interest in visiting Cowper's garden and found his summer house preserved exactly as he left it'. Indeed it is still there today: 'Behind the house Cowper's garden and his tiny unassuming Summer House'.

Pickwick Papers, chap. 16

Letter to Lady Hesketh 25 May 1786

Letter to Joseph Hill 28 June 1785

Life 1846, vol. II p. 384

William Lucas, 1934, vol. 2, p. 450

Pevsner, *Bucks*, 1960, p. 220

A traveller in nineteenth-century Holland noted their attractions in that country; while on a journey by barge 'We passed by a large number of country villas, every one surrounded by small canals, and adorned with a flowery Dutch garden, and a summer-house for smoking and tea-drinking, at the edge of the *ditch-water* . . . . Yet the neat appearance of these residences, the curious *parterres*, the green shutters, etc. are quite attractive and agreeable'.

Memoirs of J. J. Gurney, Norwich, 1855, vol. 2, p. 249

Scale of feet:

In the pages which follow I have described in detail most of the summer houses which were standing in 1963, and have illustrated my descriptions with sketches, sketch plans all to the same scale, and cuttings from old plans of the town. In a few instances there have been historical notes to add, very occasionally an indication of the date of the building. Since 1963 some of these summer houses have decayed further and others have gone completely. However within the last few years more attention has been given to the few that have survived so that there is hope that they may continue for many years yet to illuminate this little-known backwater of Kendal history.

Number 1 on map

The most prominent situation overlooking the town is occupied by Kendal's finest summer house. It belongs to the earlier group and is one of the very few in use and kept in good order. It stands on the south-east corner of Bowling Fell on a rocky bluff with an open view over the whole eastern horizon. In 1770 the site was shown as part of the open Fell, but by 1787 the enclosing

Todd, 1787, showing the garden and summer house to the left of Bowling Fell, before the house Airey Cliff was built.

1 — *Bowling Fell.*

walls, planting, paths and summer house were complete as well as the adjacent public paths and steps from Garth Head up to Bowling Fell. The addition a century later of the house Airey Cliff, named after its builder, did little to alter the pattern of the old garden or to diminish the effect of the old summer house. This octagonal building has three round-headed windows with a gothick pattern of glazing bars, irregularly placed round the upper room. Here

Todd, 1787, showing the early bowling green on the Fell.

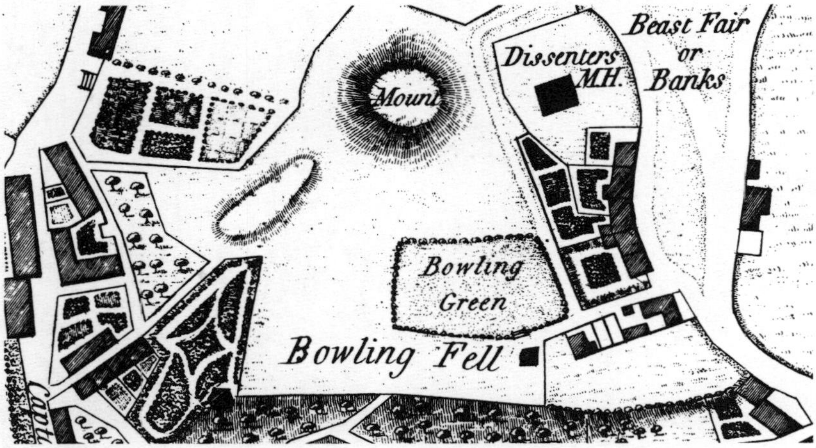

Wood, 1833 showing the later bowling green and summer house at Bank View

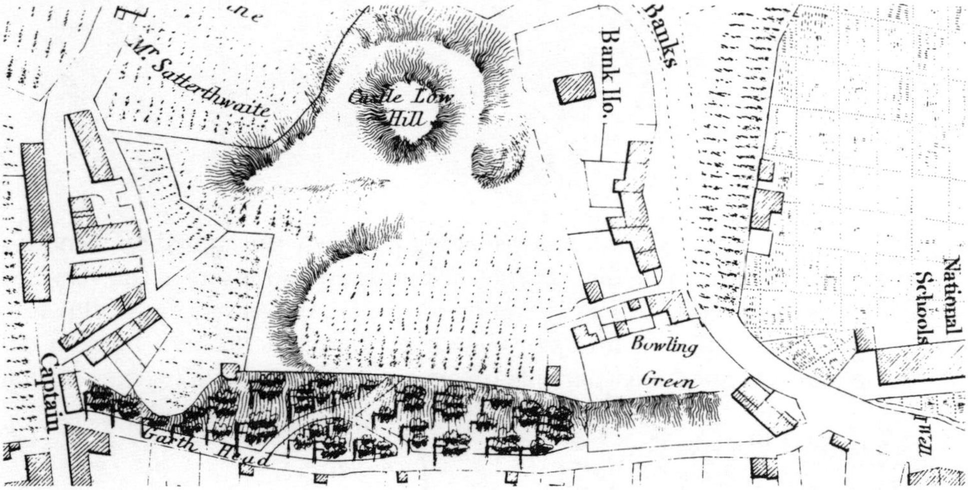

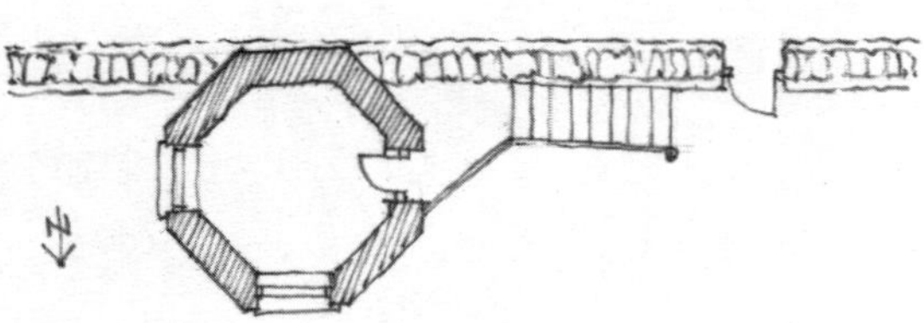

2 — *Bank View.*

there is a fireplace, a small alcove and a round-headed door at the head of the outside steps. Below it is a low room lit by a single small window. The slate roof rises from a timber cornice to a decorative finial at the apex; it formerly covered a segmental coved ceiling in the upper room. The building is a handsome and fitting complement to its situation.

ee Todd's lan

ee Wood's lan

Jumber 2 n map

There has been a bowling green on this Fell for many years. One is shown on the plan of 1770 and again in 1787 on the open bailey of Castle Howe, and beside the latter an indication of a small building presumably associated with the game. By 1833 these had gone and had been replaced by an enclosed green and the building shown in the sketch. This green in turn ceased to be used after a new green was established on Tenterfell in 1866; it became a garden with a summer house, retaining in the lower room ranks of compart-

Bank View.

ments for keeping the players' bowls. The upper room had a large window facing north overlooking the green and was reached by steps built out from the boundary wall. It lacked some of the facilities of a true summer house as it had no fireplace, no wall-cupboard, and no distant view, but it made an excellent summer house all the same. It was swept away in 1966 when a new bungalow was built in the garden.

Bank View.

There are traces of a dozen summer houses below the wall which separates Bowling Fell and Garth Head from the gardens of houses on Highgate but only one complete building, situated behind the Marvic Hotel. This was once the house of Hugh Holme, deputy recorder and attorney-at-law, was rebuilt at his death in 1770, and was bought in 1817 by Justice James Wilson: such were the people who then lived in Highgate. When the property was put up for sale in 1766 the advertisement described the house in estate agent's familiar and customary detail and then went on to give the first dated reference to a summer house: 'The garden is walled round, planted with a variety of fruit trees, and terminates with a pleasant summer house on an eminence that commands an extensive view of the Town and Country adjacent'. This building we no longer see, but a more fashionable and less substantial replacement whose walls of unfamiliar brick in two colours support a slate

Number 3 on map

Curwen p. 141

ibid.

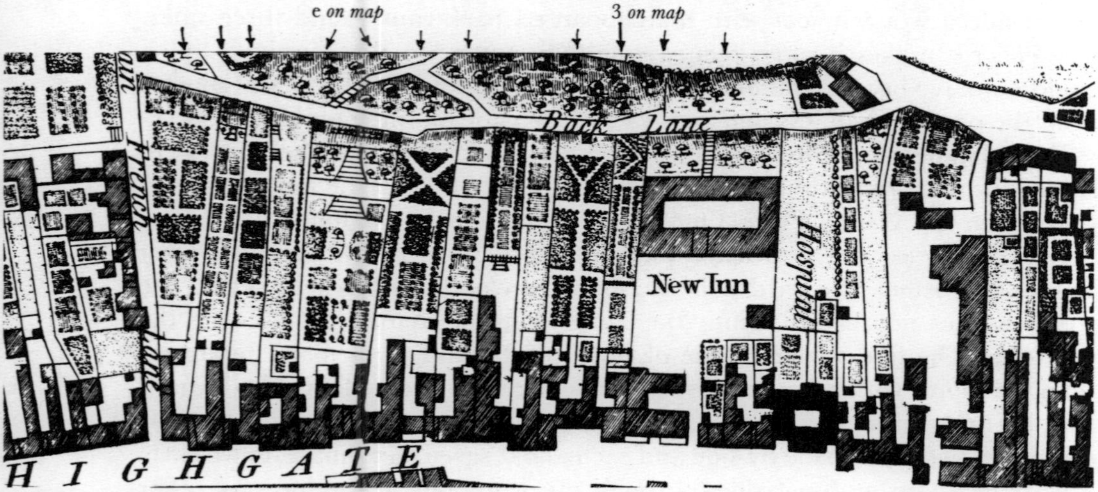

Todd's plan of 1787: the arrows indicate the location of summer houses at the back of Highgate properties; some built after the plan was drawn.

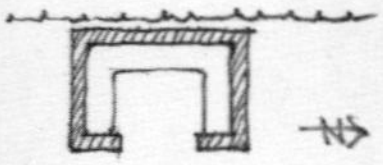

3 — *Highgate.*

roof edged with bargeboards and finial of disproportionate size, a sight familiar in the cottage-orné of the earlier part of the last century. Its alcove, for this is not an enclosed room, is framed by a Tudor arch lined with a timber moulding, and inside a wooden seat with matchboarded back runs round three sides. The effect it makes is more picturesque than any other that survives, but it could not have been useful to its owner in the traditional way. It dates though from the period when less demand was being made on these buildings.

Number 4 on map

From Highgate northwards through the centre of the town there is less to show, but until recently there were the remains of two on the higher ground centred on the Market Place. One stood behind Old Bank House, which was built in 1789 for the Lancaster Bank to the designs of the local architect Francis Webster. The garden house followed closely the pattern set by the street house, notably in using the same unusual shaped lintels over the windows. The fine ashlar façade of this little building was more important than the rooms within, and it seems to have been considered first as an elegant feature to terminate a garden vista, only second as accommodation. It contained two rooms side by side and each about seven feet square, one clearly a working room with a ladder through the trap-door to the loft, the other fitted out with a seat and a relatively ornate plaster cornice. There was no fireplace however, and the chimney which appeared over the back gable served one of the outbuildings in the yard below. Thus the only summer house

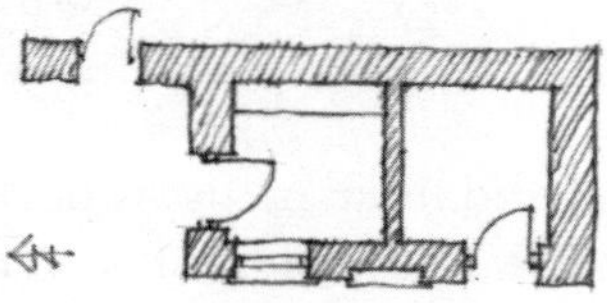

4 — *Stricklandgate.*

which might perhaps be attributable to an architect combined in one elegant composition the functions of architectural screen, garden shed, seed loft, chimney stack and garden room. The assumption is that it was built very soon after the house and perhaps by 1800. Within the last few years it has been demolished, and the garden is a car park.

umber 5
ı map

Immediately opposite across Stricklandgate there stood another summer house, one with a more complicated history than most. At the time of its demolition in 1970 it presented an interesting problem of reconstruction: it was then a derelict outhouse which had evidently seen better and more gracious times. In fact it began life as an outhouse, to which was later applied

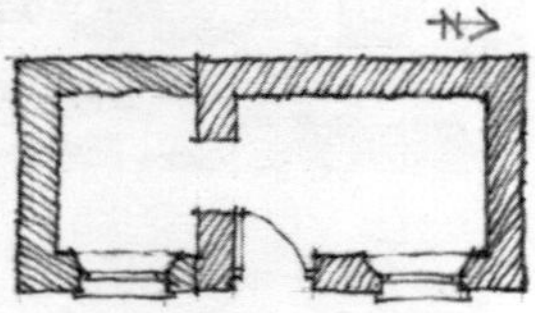

floor plan: the later extension is to the left.

5 — *Stricklandgate.*

a stucco façade and traceried windows. It may be assumed that a summer house interior had been applied as well, though the remaining evidence was negligible. At a later date it was extended re-using the same large decorative windows which defined its genteel function. The drawing shows a reconstruction of the building in its earlier days as a summer house, when it gave a view over the small garden and across the valley to Benson Knott; the plan shows it in 1970. Perhaps, for people looking back from the garden, it served also as a decorative screen between garden and kitchen yard of the old and unfashionable house, a house which was occupied for a few years from 1845 by Cornelius Nicholson, annalist of Kendal.

ırwen
347

Todd 1787: Summer House number 6 is in the garden to the right of Blackhall Croft.

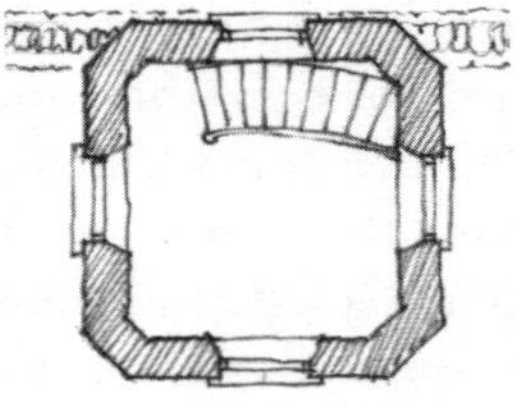

above.

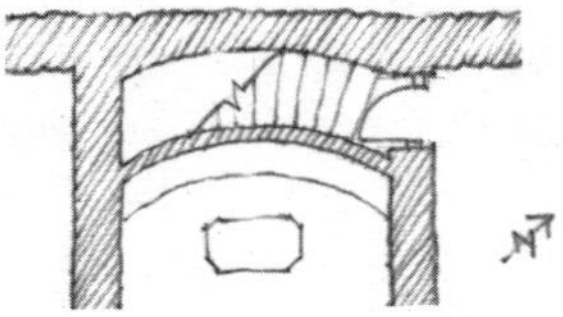

6 — *Stramongate. below.*

To the east along a tongue of higher ground was the old footpath to Stramongate known as Blackhall Croft. Todd's map of 1787 shows the house beside the Croft, which had been built in 1786 and described as 'a capital house', in which a bank was established in 1788. Behind it were the usual outbuildings, a long garden planted with four parallel rows of trees and at the end a summer house. This too was a capital building, an irregular octagon or bevelled square of two storeys, an upper room over an alcove. The alcove was furnished with a square marble table supported on a single heavy stone baluster; the curved plaster partition behind it concealed the staircase, the only internal one found in Kendal. The room upstairs had four large sash windows, two latterly built up, but apparently there was no fireplace despite the excellence of the building in other respects. There was a cellar though, which was re-discovered while the building was being demolished in 1963 to

Curwen p. 398

Number 6 on map

6 — *Stramongate.*

make way for the new Blackhall Road. Another casualty of that same road was a much more ordinary building nearby, whose raised floor and two large windows lift it from the class of garden utility to a more elegant use.

umber 7
map

7 — *Stramongate.*

8 — *Wildman Street.*

umber 8
n map

Across the river by Stramongate bridge one older summer house remains behind a shop in Wildman Street, its original window looking south over Stock Beck to the Castle Hill now completely blocked by the building of Castle Street School. Further out of the town, fitted into a small garden beside the railway line, is a relatively recent two-storey summer house complete with a fireplace, fully in the old tradition.

umber 9
n map

9 — *Castle Road.*

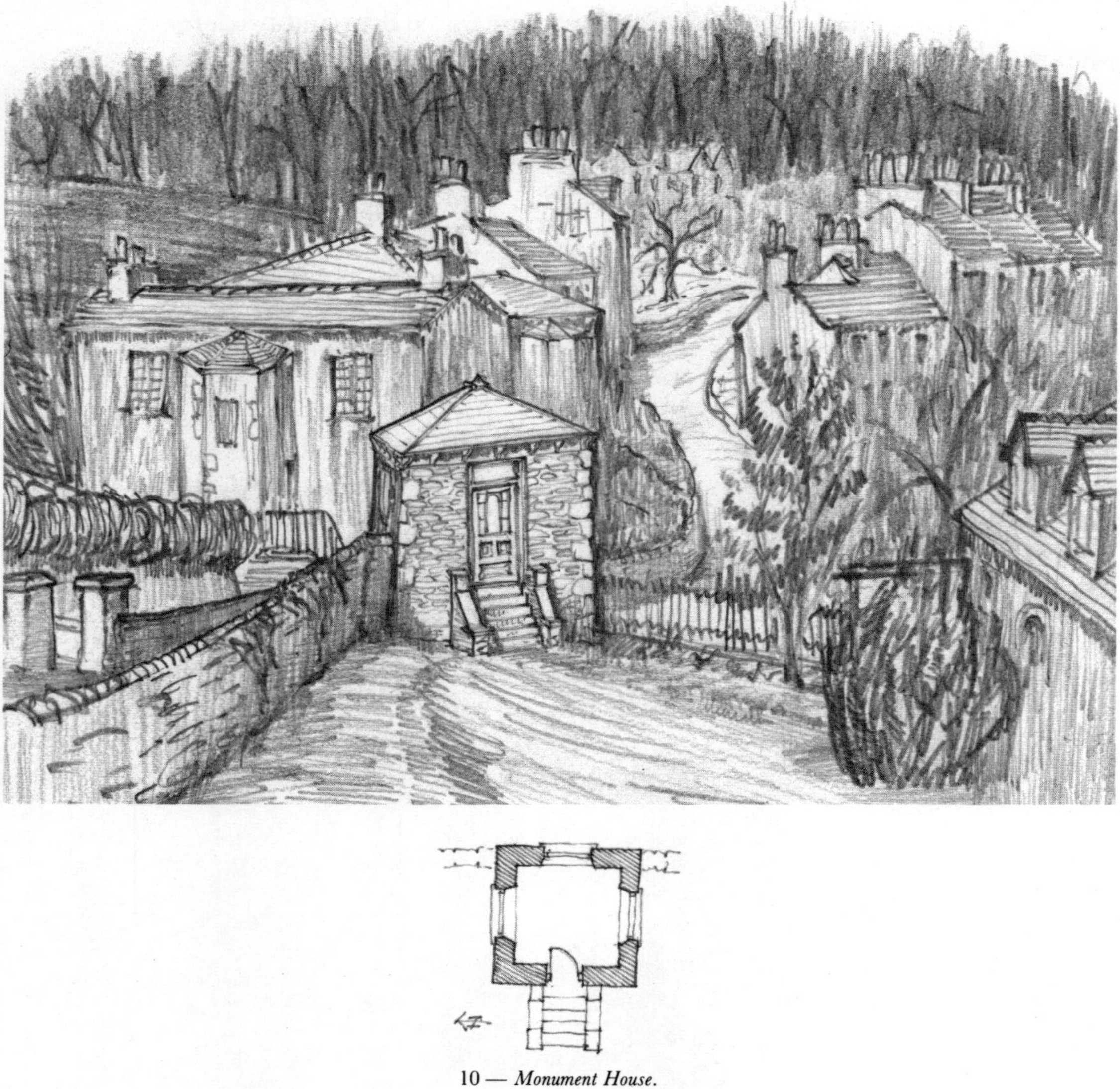

10 — *Monument House.*

Thus far we have described some of the earlier summer houses. As the nineteenth century progressed so were others built around and above the town, as well-built and as well-equipped as those earlier buildings. One is at

Number 10 on map

Monument House, in those days known as Bank House or Hill House, at the top of Beast Bank. Curwen writes of it: 'When Edward Burton, auctioneer, purchased the house, he made many considerable alterations, adding the

p 84

verandah in front, the two false wings, one on either side, [since removed] and by building a coach house and summer house at each end of the palisading'.

10 — *Monument House.*

11 — *Gulfs Road.*

It was between 1833 and 1851 that these alterations were made. The summer house occupies the highest corner of the garden beside the road where it is a prominent feature of the walk from the town up to Greenside.

Number 11 on map

Beside Miller Bridge and at the foot of Lowther Street there are several substantial houses but so far it appears there was only one summer house. It replaces an earlier and larger building of unknown use which stood at least from 1786 to 1853 overlooking the river at the foot of a long garden; it was perhaps built when this was demolished and the garden divided to make way for Gulfs Road towards the end of the last century. The precise stonework and the bright red ridge tiles belong to that period. The prospect from this low-lying summer house was of necessity one of river rather than hill; upstream to Gooseholme, downstream to Abbot Hall.

Number 12 on map

Cliff Terrace, a little way to the north of Monument House, was built between 1851 and 1853 at about the same time as a fine summer house was put up in the garden beyond. A few years later the large house called Chapel View was built in that same garden, in a very different style of architecture. The summer house stands on a terrace which runs the full length of the garden below the lane called Cliff Brow, from the house at one end to a small but decorative conservatory which once stood at the other. In front of the summer house the terrace widens out in a bow with an iron balustrade. At this level is the lower room with small round-headed windows, clearly a utilitarian work room. The upper room, reached by outside steps, is provided with everything needed for comfort and style. There are two windows to take in the considerable view, a fireplace and a tall cupboard with panelled doors, arched alcoves formed within the thickness of the wall, and over all a coved ceiling with a deeply-moulded cornice. This delightful building has been decaying for many years, but no longer: now it has been re-roofed and repaired and is enjoyed.

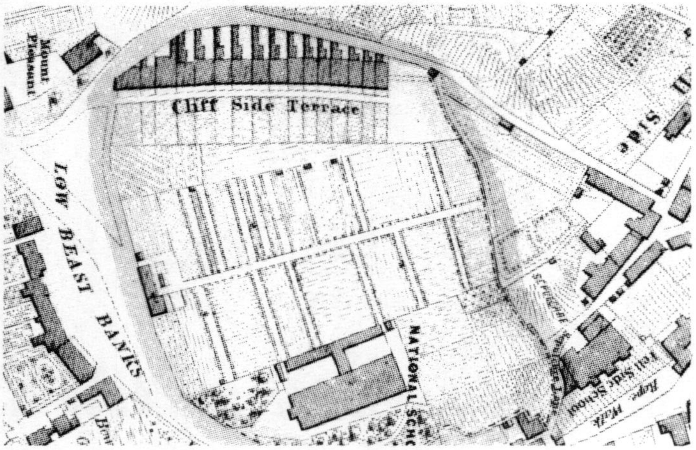

Hoggarth, 1853, showing the newly-built Cliff Side Terrace and the summer house to the right: Chapel View was later built between them.

12 — *Chapel View.*

Chapel View.

These notes may have helped us to build up a picture of the place that summer houses once held in the life of Kendal, and of their interest and variety. Yet they were little more than a passing fashion, built and bought and sold to meet the need of the time and as readily discarded when that time had passed. Now after many years of neglect a few flourish again and once more offer pleasure, to those who find them unexpectedly as well as to their owners, sitting watching the light of the evening sun on the eastern fells.